THE PROBLEM WITH

BLOOPERS OF INVENTION

EARLY CAMERAS

OOPS!

Gareth Stevens
PUBLISHING

BY RYAN NAGELHOUT

Please visit our website, www.garethstevens.com. For a free color catalog of all our high-quality books, call toll free 1-800-542-2595 or fax 1-877-542-2596.

Library of Congress Cataloging-in-Publication Data

Nagelhout, Ryan.
The problem with early cameras / by Ryan Nagelhout.
p. cm. — (Bloopers of invention)
Includes index.
ISBN 978-1-4824-2756-1 (pbk.)
ISBN 978-1-4824-2757-8 (6 pack)
ISBN 978-1-4824-2758-5 (library binding)
1. Cameras — History — Juvenile literature. 2. Inventions — Juvenile literature. I. Nagelhout, Ryan. II. Title.
TR250.N34 2016
770—d23

First Edition

Published in 2016 by
Gareth Stevens Publishing
111 East 14th Street, Suite 349
New York, NY 10003

Copyright © 2016 Gareth Stevens Publishing

Designer: Sarah Liddell
Editor: Ryan Nagelhout

Photo credits: Cover, p. 1 Hulton Archive/Stringer/Getty Images; p. 5 General Photographic Agency/Stringer/Getty Images; p. 7 (camera obscura diagram) Ellin Beltz/Wikimedia Commons; p. 7 (projection) Gampe/Wikimedia Commons; p. 9 (main) Frances DEMANGE/Contributor/Getty Images; p. 9 (photograph) Ed g2s/Wikimedia Commons; p. 11 (Niépce) Jean-Luc PETIT/Contributor/Getty Images; p. 11 (Daguerre) GianniG46/Wikimedia Commons; pp. 13 (plate camera), 15 (photograph) Science & Society Picture Library/Contributor/Getty Images; p. 13 (Archer) Svajcr/Wikimedia Commons; p. 15 (Eastman) American Stock Archive/Contributor/Getty Images; p. 15 (camera) Royal Photographic Society/Contributor/Getty Images; p. 17 (reels) Fabio Pagani/Shutterstock.com; p. 17 (double exposure) Smallbot/Wikimedia Commons; p. 19 (camera) Bubba73/Wikimedia Commons; p. 19 (photograph) Tobatrance/Wikimedia Commons; p. 21 Kurt Stricker/Moment/Getty Images.

Printed in the United States of America

CPSIA compliance information: Batch #CS15GS: For further information contact Gareth Stevens, New York, New York at 1-800-542-2595.

CONTENTS

Words in the glossary appear in **bold** type the first time they are used in the text.

PICTURE PERFECT?

Today's smart cameras can give you amazing pictures with the touch of a button. Even cell phones and tablet computers have cameras that take great pictures you can share with all your friends.

Early camera technology wasn't always so easy to use. People made plenty of mistakes while trying to invent a good camera. Images were often turned the wrong way and many different **chemicals** were needed to make the pictures. It took a long time for people to figure out how to make a good camera!

OOPS!

Today's cameras are easy to use. If you wanted to take a picture in the early 1800s, though, you had to invent a camera for yourself!

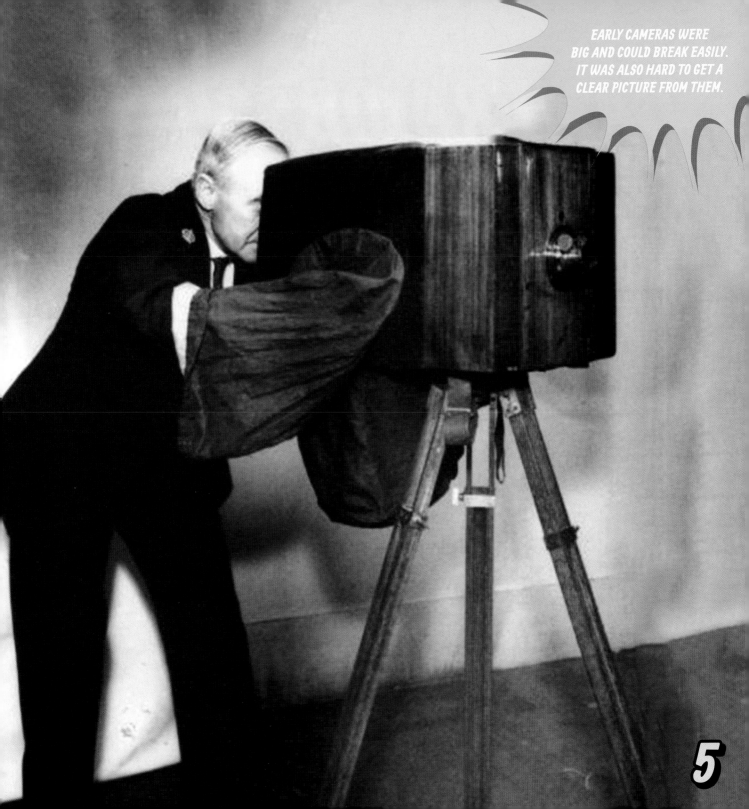

EARLY CAMERAS WERE BIG AND COULD BREAK EASILY. IT WAS ALSO HARD TO GET A CLEAR PICTURE FROM THEM.

CAMERA OBSCURA

The first "camera" was made with a tiny hole! Called the camera obscura, Latin for "dark chamber," the first camera was just that: a dark room with covered windows. A hole let in light from the outside, which could **project** an image onto a wall.

Camera obscuras were first used to help artists. The image that came through the pinhole could be traced and helped painters create art that looked closer to real life. During the 16th century, the device was made much smaller and became a movable box.

OOPS!

Light rays **reverse** themselves when going through the small hole, so the image early camera obscuras made would be upside down and reversed! Camera obscuras later used lenses and mirrors to help **orient** the image the right way.

projection from a camera obscura

USING A CAMERA OBSCURA

image

hole

light

mirror

FIRST PHOTOGRAPH

By 1826, French inventor Joseph-Nicéphore Niépce made the first **permanent** photo with bitumen, which hardened when **exposed** to light. He then removed the unexposed areas to get a negative, or inverse of an image, a process he called "heliography."

A few years later, French artist Jacques Daguerre discovered that Niépce was trying to use light to create plates that could be inked to make prints. The two decided to work together to create a new kind of photography, or "light writing."

OOPS!

Niépce also created the first "negative" in 1816 with a camera obscura and paper coated with silver salts. The image disappeared when exposed to daylight because the paper turned black!

DAGUERRE FOUND OUT ABOUT NIÉPCE'S WORK BECAUSE THEY USED THE SAME LENS MAKER IN PARIS!

camera used by Niépce

first permanent photograph

9

THE DAGUERREOTYPE

Niépce died in 1833, before Daguerre perfected their work and invented the daguerreotype. Created in 1837, daguerreotypes made photographs by putting iodine on silver-plated copper sheets to make them **sensitive** to light. Using a warm vapor of the element mercury, the image "**developed**" on the sheets to make a photo.

Daguerre first tried to make money off his method, but later published it so others could make daguerreotypes. This helped others make new kinds of light-sensitive photographs with different chemicals.

OOPS!

Mercury is a metal that is liquid at room temperature and can be harmful to humans. People who come into contact with mercury can get poisoned!

DAGUERREOTYPES TOOK ABOUT 15 MINUTES TO EXPOSE, MAYBE LONGER!

daguerreotype of Jacques Daguerre

Joseph-Nicéphore Niépce

11

PLATE CAMERAS

In 1851, English inventor Frederick Scott Archer improved on Daguerre's design by using a plate of glass covered in light-sensitive chemicals to capture an image. The seven-step process wasn't much easier than the daguerreotype, but it was much cheaper. It soon became the most popular way to make photographs.

The plates were only sensitive to light when wet, which meant they had to be used as soon as possible. A **darkroom** could be set up in a tent, railway car, or even a wagon to help develop Archer's plate-glass photos.

OOPS!

People had to sit still for a long time to get their picture taken. That's why many of them looked so angry! If they couldn't keep the same face, the picture would be ruined.

ARCHER'S CAMERA MADE A CLEAR NEGATIVE IMAGE THAT WAS USED TO MAKE PHOTOS.

plate photograph of Frederick Scott Archer

13

EASTMAN AND KODAK

The invention of dry plates helped cameras become cheaper and more **portable**. Then, in 1888, American inventor George Eastman created a new kind of camera called the Kodak.

It was the first camera made to use a **flexible** film camera roll. The original Kodak was a wooden box with film made from something called cellulose inside. It could be used with a simple press of a button. Each box had enough film for 100 photos.

OOPs!

The first Kodak camera required customers to bring their entire camera back to Eastman to develop their photos! The film roll had to be cut in pieces and put on plates to be developed.

THE KODAK CAMERA HELPED CHANGE PHOTOGRAPHY FROM AN EXPENSIVE HOBBY TO SOMETHING ALMOST ANYONE COULD AFFORD TO DO.

George Eastman

photograph taken by first Kodak camera

15

ROLLS AND ROLLS

Interchangeable rolls of film were added as cameras became smaller. Different types of film at different sizes could create different-sized photos. In 1900, Kodak first sold the Brownie camera. It cost $1 for the camera and 15 cents for each roll of film. Early film was made with a chemical called nitrate, which was highly **flammable**!

As film rolls improved in quality and size, a new kind of photography was created. Inventor Thomas Edison used the technology to string images together to create motion pictures, or movies.

OOPs! Sometimes film would accidentally be used twice. This was called double exposure and made for some wild photos.

double-exposed film

17

COLOR AND INSTANT CAMERAS

Photos were first made in color during the early 20th century as film improved. Cameras were also made with their own darkroom! In 1947, American inventor Edwin Land created the instant camera with the Polaroid process.

This combined the exposure and development process into one, and cameras spit out a "Polaroid." The photo started as a blank image that became a photo in about a minute. This meant you didn't have to take your film to a photo center to get it developed.

OOPS!

Polaroid cameras didn't have negatives, which meant you couldn't make pictures over and over again. You couldn't make copies, you had to take another picture!

POLAROID CAMERAS WERE THE FASTEST WAY TO GET PICTURES DEVELOPED BECAUSE THE PHOTO DEVELOPED INSTANTLY.

Polaroid instant photo

19

DIGITAL PHOTOGRAPHY

Today, we've taken the film right out of the camera altogether! Digital cameras still have a lens to capture images, but there's no film or plate to put them on. Instead, computer memory cards store the images in bits and bytes. Digital cameras were invented in the 1980s, but weren't popular until the 21st century.

OOPs! If you lose a memory card or your computer breaks, you can lose all your digital photos!

Most cell phones also have tiny cameras inside that let us edit images after they're captured. What do you think the camera of tomorrow will look like?

MENU

25" 32 101-0620 CF

INFO.

RAW+L

GLOSSARY

chemical: matter that can be mixed with other matter to cause changes

darkroom: a lightproof room used to develop and print photos

develop: to make or become clear gradually or in detail

expose: to let light fall on something

flammable: capable of being easily set on fire and burning quickly

flexible: able to bend without breaking

interchangeable: able to be put in place of each other

orient: to arrange in a certain position

permanent: lasting for a long time

portable: able to be moved or carried

project: to throw forward onto a surface

reverse: to turn completely about or upside down

sensitive: capable of responding to something

FOR MORE INFORMATION

BOOKS

Raum, Elizabeth. *The History of the Camera*. Chicago, IL: Heinemann Library, 2008.

Richter, Joanne. *Inventing the Camera*. New York, NY: Crabtree Publishing, 2006.

Trueit, Trudi Strain. *The Camera*. New York, NY: Franklin Watts, 2006.

WEBSITES

Creating Effective Camera Obscuras
pinholephotography.org/camera%20obscurer.htm
Learn how you can make your own camera obscura.

The First Photograph
hrc.utexas.edu/exhibitions/permanent/firstphotograph/
Find out more about Joseph-Nicéphore Niépce and how he made the first permanent photograph.

INDEX